Patched & Repaired

26 Poems
Marcia C. Harvey

Copyright © 2016 by Marcia Claire Harvey.
All rights reserved.
ISBN-13: 978-0692564998
ISBN-10: 0692564993

Dodo Press
Paso Robles
California
www.wayofthedodo.org

*For E. and H.,
and Brown Owls everywhere.*

Contents

Unutterable / 1
R. S. V. P. / 2
1.16.10 / 3
The Year of the Rat Begins / 4
Fable, Maybe / 5
Half as Much / 6
Moonshine / 8
Ode to a Painting of a Lemon by Édouard Manet / 9
Above All Else, Grief Floods / 10
The Smoke-Scent of the Night-Time Neighbor / 11
The Old Car / 12
Two Views from a Tiny Chair / 15
Found Poems from <u>Fruits Basket 2</u> / 16
Winter Tide Robins / 18
Found Poem from "Abandoned
      House at Twilight" / 20
The Jaguar Man and Woman / 21
The Writer is Trying to Enchant / 22
How to Explain Pictures to an Old Lawyer / 23
Waiting Room / 24
The Three Fates / 25
Partial Poem / 26
Things To Do for Sculptures / 27
Tell the Future / 28
I Often Wonder What Became of Him / 30
Each Night / 32
A Blur, a Niche, a Fault / 33

Patched & Repaired

UNUTTERABLE

I traced a thousand lines with my nail.

You said: They are chasing a hare.
I saw only black wings on gilded air.

I looked again,
to read the un-written.

You cast me a shadow at the corner,
as proof, at the end,
of the hare.

R. S. V. P.

I thought there was a barn.

No one seemed to recall it.

I am sure there was a pond:
A green pond with algae and leaves floating.

I am sure of that, that green pond.

There was a green pond.

We could even,
probably,
agree on that.

1.16.10

Here, so early

is the first wildflower of this year, nigh decade.

He gave it to me; a Heliotrope- a Phacelia.

It has that wild sweetness, that scent you can't seem to get enough of in your inhalation,
but that even that less than full not enough amount is
too much
too sweet
too vertiginous, too live, too lush, too full, too almost the end;

too much loss is in it.

THE YEAR OF THE RAT BEGINS

The world with two skies.

Today I have the eye of the golden eagle,
And I can see around the bend.

FABLE, MAYBE

A poem blew by on the breeze just now;
like the poets say they do.

It rattled and loosed the leaves on a grove of trees.

A House Finch noticed it.

It lifted some dry stalks and
whirled them downslope,
leaving the scent of the dry stream in its wake.

Or, it might have been
a fable.

HALF AS MUCH

There is a towering cactus;
long wavering limbs of blue, grey, green.
Cacto super gigante.

Growing at the end of one road and the middle of
another,
and it blooms
at night
in heat
in summer
in street light.

Milkmoon trumpets
Sound from greygreen arms.

A boy drove his car through the night
one hundred miles an hour
through a near telephone pole,

that carries the electricity that lights our
night dark rooms

and the lights went out
and a fire burned
and the cactus burned
and slumped
and ashed.

And blooms were
beaten off and branches broken.

MOONSHINE

In this moonrise;
one hundred such shines,
a thousand evenings,
one million cricket chirps
distilled.

I ask my son,
8, do you remember the lines of ore cars?
Just, what, two years ago?

No, he does not. This
moon, for him, is one of
a few, containing perhaps
a dozen evenings.

My moon holds the shine
of lightning,
of one thousand egrets,
of countless pearls.

ODE TO A PAINTING OF A LEMON BY ÉDOUARD MANET

That yellow, that
chalky tartness.

Such desire. To pick it up,
to have it, to know it.

To possess all the impossible darkness of space around-
not brushed, but inlaid
into walnut wood;
mahogany.

Illuminated from where?
From here.

It is coming together.
It is coming apart.

ABOVE ALL ELSE, GRIEF FLOODS

Part I

I don't keep files anymore.

No ledgers, no journals.
I leave the checkbook to itself.

Part II

I save and sort:

a torn scrap with two words: lush, generous.
A small drawing of a Christmas pudding.
A two and one half inch long list:

> paint can opener
> piece of wire bent into a paper clip
> funnel
> sweet tart
> a tiny chair
> spirograph wheel.

THE SMOKE-SCENT OF
THE NIGHT-TIME NEIGHBOR

At the late of night; sometimes,
the middle- no sounds and no
wind; I smell the smoke of the neighbor-
it is just her and I for a minute and then
come creeping the others.

My Great-grandfather and his pipe, and my
Granduncles, too.
And my Grandfather and his cigars, and my
Grandmother and her cigarettes,
and my teenage self, and Yvonne,
whom kinfolk come to see by the dozen.

And then even more crowd into the stillness:
Old teachers, a Godmother;
Painters, and bad boys,
patient people setting on stoops;
insomniacs from all around the world,
drifters, and wharf-rat poets.

And we are all together in this,
in the night, in the scent in the dark of
smoke.

THE OLD CAR

The old car is growing lichen. She will not turn
over, she had to be pushed to a new
place in the yard when we got a new old car.

I emptied her glove box, her side door pockets, her
secret compartments:

A first aid kit, snow chains.
A rubber iguana.
A very fine white heron plume.
½ a dozen black feathers. Raven, or crow.

Loose parts, screws. Fuses.
Papers, and notes:
    "I went to make bait at the south end of the
    launch ramp. B-RIGHT BACK-"
Another one, with drawings of people, buildings, fish:
    "I want to see you badly."

Master's program class schedule:
    01. Grad. Painting arrgt., etc.
A paper folded with dried brown petals inside: "with
love, of course."
A blue hair comb.
A medallion from The League of the Sacred Heart.
A wrinkled picture postcard of the Hollywood Hills.

A memorial card for burial at sea:
        3 miles off the coast of San Diego, Ca., June 7th,
        1996, aboard the America II.

A map to the Lochsa Lodge, Idaho.
Track guide.
Bird checklist.
Refuge maps.
A blue jay feather.
The Indian on a Tootsie Pop wrapper.

A seed pod from a magnolia.
Sedimentary rocks.
Flint knapped chert.
Moonstones. Quartzes.
A heart shaped stone.
Coins. Washers.
A pregnancy test wand: positive.
Bay leaves. Nails.

Dun scraps of the front seat leather.
A Mephisto writing pencil No. 4.
A Mary Oliver playbill:
        (She said she'd had the good fortune in
        life to always have jobs that she did not
        care about, which left her mind free for
        the task of writing poetry.)

We drove her all the way to the Atlantic; over the Mississippi, all over the deserts of the Southwest. The forests of the Northwest. The high peaks of the Continental Divide. The Redwoods, the Sierras, the dunes, the bluffs. To Butte, Montana. To motels, hot springs, beaches. Camping, drive-in movies, the Grand Canyon's North Rim. The Vermillion Cliffs. Lava beds. Foothills, lowlands, pastures. Snowy passes, comet-lit skies. Shallow lakes, vast tracts of cacti, mesquite. Mossy riversides, shaded bosques. Memphis, Tennessee. Kansas City.

A fitting end for her, for Mrs. Hortensia Plum (aka Imelda "Hot-Box" Vavoom) would be for John Chamberlain to make a fine sculpture of her, that we could put by the hen house, and watch her rust as the years continue to go by. Or, we could plant her with geraniums and sweet peas. We could have her rebuilt; give her new paint, new rubber, new upholstery, an engine, new rims. I could wear my gray hair in a bun, and a calico dress, and I could drive her in parades in ten, twenty years, when even a car born in 1986 would be a rare antique: she'd be 40 or 50 years old and people would say "gee, is that what cars used to look like?!"

TWO VIEWS FROM A TINY CHAIR

They were cautious, besprinkled.
They may not have seen me.

Hemmingway's place in Idaho.
I am thinking of you there,
now, too. Bothered by the
pines and their dizzying shadows.

FOUND POEMS FROM <u>FRUITS BASKET 2</u>, by Natsuki Takaya

One

Pitter-patter
Clatter.

Crunchies.
Clunk
Ta-da!

Cringe.

Two

Dazed, dash, whack
(badum badum) wham.

(Teary stare)
crackle crackle
    (burning rage)
Slip bam, dash wham.

Blush, spark, turn, shoop
Twitch.

Bang, -clatter, -crash, -bang

Pop, grab, poof!

Tumble, bonk, dump.

WINTER TIDE ROBINS

I

They swooped out of an
orange cloud bank,
one storm-edged sunset: A winter flock of Robins.

Late afternoons they gather to greet the gloaming.
A noisome fluttering of hundreds,
with chuffing clucks and sharp zeet-tweets,
together with a shuddering of wings
colliding with leaves, like a window shade
accordioning up and down; like a
lace-edged Spanish fan, shutting abruptly: Rapido.

They take hours to arrive and settle- to find their
branches. Boughs begin to bend with their weight.
Invisible in the leaves, they are shoulder to shoulder and
cheek to cheek: A dense packing of red breasts.
The sounds fade and the sallying birds dwindle.

Where are they all day?
Where were they this time last year?

II

Where are they all day?
A widely spaced pack, they are legion.

Sixty flutter in from the North and settle
briefly, in a tree. Then another wave from
the East. The first group lights out, and
another hundred approach, curving from
the West.

The dusk sky is spattered
in all directions with Robins.

This flock, it might be much larger than the yard-
They may reach as far as the main road.
Maybe over the ridge, across the stream.
Maybe as far as the Salinas.
They might stretch eight miles to town.
They might be over the coast; they might be in the
desert: Monterey and Inyokern.

A poet, at the sea, begins a haiku about their rufous
chests. In town, a folksinger pens a ballad to their
numbers, and miles and miles away,
at the unknown edge of their winter-gathering,
a novel's first chapter commences:
The winter robins darted over the house.

FOUND POEM FROM "ABANDONED HOUSE
   AT TWILIGHT"- a Charles Burchfield drawing

Cold light
frog songs
new grass shoots.

THE JAGUAR MAN AND WOMAN

The Jaguar Man and Woman are dying;
They have no young.

They prowl the shore together, limping down the wharf
on arthritic hips.

"Are they really part wild cat?" I ask the former mayor.
"Oh yes," she says, "oh yes."

Returning home this day, they will kill a newspaper
woman and a fisherman, before they are shot. The
fisherman will drown trying to save his ex-wife, as he
always knew he would.
The journalist will be struck by a gaff.

The waves are made of tears, and the boat shed is filled
with owls and linnets.
And the waves are made of tears.

THE WRITER IS TRYING TO ENCHANT

Fate, destiny,

time, forward and back- a canned shandy on the Isle of Wight-
a message:
(in a novel, or a bottle; a deus ex machina)

Stay under the spell.

HOW TO EXPLAIN PICTURES TO AN OLD LAWYER

I was explaining pictures to a tiny, old, wizened lawyer.
I said "see, here, come close to the canvas- There?
Do you see how you have to come up here to where you
can only see the painting?
Nothing else in the room?

Now, you feel surprise, as there is no one here, no one in
the picture- Who is this a picture of?
You become a little lost, a little nervous.
What is this a picture of? It is so large,
it is bigger than you-
It could hold you,
swallow you up,
absorb you.

It is you.
The picture's space, its nothingness has left.
A place for you. The picture's meaning is you.
You are the painting.

WAITING ROOM

In the waiting area,
You said you sold cars,
Zipping up your jacket.

I said: Yes, I've seen you around.
I'll make it easy for you to sell me one.
I'll be a 'close talker,' stepping very close.

You left.

You later returned, to sit at my side.

THE THREE FATES
for Kim.

To begin, we will have tea, and you will tell me everything he said.

Then, we will get a cup of espresso, and a bit of chocolate, and I'll ask you what you said.

Next, we will go to a bar, and get a booth; very dark, very quiet. We will order a bottle of something womanly; sherry or prosecco, and we will drink to all the years of our lost innocence, and toast 'to vulnerability,' and 'to courage,' and 'to hope.'

"It is no harm: Pay no attention to it!"
  -Wm. Saroyan

PARTIAL POEM

I am digging this ditch, see,
and looking for
something to fill it with.

An elephant hair bracelet
A lacy pair of your grandmother's gloves
A pink velvet collar
A dish I made
A hat embroidered with gold threads and glass pearls
All these damned days of the week.

THINGS TO DO FOR SCULPTURES

Things to do for sculptures:

decorate the cart

tie and secure the nest,
make a red ladder

wind woolen threads around wooden heart

attach wheeled legs

seal the seam;
wrap with beaten wire.

TELL THE FUTURE

I wanted to write.

A big, rambling poem.
A capacious clattering of lines, stanzas and pages.
A poem that would tell the future.
And the past. All about the past.

To give it to the future.

This wasn't here then, it was open;
you could see the sky.
There was a dirt road there, and a little path.
A tree grew just there.
This used to be a field; with flowers in the spring.

It is the story of loss.

You lose your shirt.
Your house, your wife.
Your looks, your youth.
Your keys.

Your loved ones.

It is the story of loss.

Your stone cairns, your dusty libraries,
museums and attics.

It is the story of loss.

I OFTEN WONDER WHAT BECAME OF HIM

I often wonder what became of him.

You need never again wonder what became of
him, or anyone. In fact, you are forbidden
to wonder. You must face all facts, all truths,
in color, in compressed stereo, with lightning speed.

You are not allowed even the transitional courtesy
of a sentence beginning: Since I last saw you....

No, you need never wonder, or suppose.
Or be happily convinced that he is a jubilant dj
on the last FM station in Ohio.
Or, imagine that he is still making
strange piles of clay heads, breaking hearts with élan,
and an echo of your last words clinging to his collar.

You cannot figure him as homesteading up in Alaska,
building a shingled cabin that is going on 18 years now.
You cannot wish that he were near enough
to bring your car to him, to repair, with greasy,
intelligent hands.

You cannot suddenly see him, in crisp detail,
explaining Turner's skies to a lecture hall full of
Liverpuddlians.

You cannot fancy that you will return one day, to find
him still piloting vaporetto in Venice.

No, you will have to know, one way or another,
of their divorces, failures, and careers;
as real estate brokers,
data shunters,
code-pushers,
production assistants,
motivational speakers,
addicts,
mountain bike riders:
Cubicled, aging,
in late model cars,
with nothing new to say at all.

EACH NIGHT

Each night, I lie next to the pages of the pale king

sometimes I knit,
or look at French recipes

in the morning, the pages flip again

I think of why you'd leave a suitcase full of chapters
why anyone would not bury or burn them

I think: whose book is it, anyway

I think: the inheritor of the suitcase

I think: I will erase all my words.

A BLUR, A NICHE, A FAULT

I will listen for you.
I will wear a hat.

I will finish your unfinished manuscript

www.ingramcontent.com/pod-product-compliance
Lightning Source LLC
Chambersburg PA
CBHW021001090426
42736CB00010B/1417